Copyright © 2024 by Chris Williams

All rights reserved.

No portion of this book may be reproduced in any form without written permission from the publisher or author, except as permitted by U.S. copyright law.

This publication is designed to provide accurate and authoritative information in regard to the subject matter covered. It is sold with the understanding that neither the author nor the publisher is engaged in rendering legal, investment, accounting or other professional services. While the publisher and author have used their best efforts in preparing this book, they make no representations or warranties with respect to the accuracy or completeness of the contents of this book and specifically disclaim any implied warranties of merchantability or fitness for a particular purpose. No warranty may be created or extended by sales representatives or written sales materials. The advice and strategies contained herein may not be suitable for your situation. You should consult with a professional when appropriate. Neither the publisher nor the author shall be liable for any loss of profit or any other commercial damages, including but not limited to special, incidental, consequential, personal, or other damages.

Book Cover by Red Squirrel Publishing Limited

Illustrations by Red Squirrel Publishing Limited

First edition 2024

Contents

1. Introduction — 1
   Welcome Aboard!
      Why Cruise?
      Who Is This Book For?
      What You'll Discover

2. Cruising 101 — 3
   The Basics
      What to Expect on Your First Cruise
      Cruise Lingo for Newbies

3. Choosing Your Perfect Cruise — 6
      Finding the Right Cruise for You
      Booking Your Cruise

4. Preparing for Your Adventure — 10
      Countdown to Cruise Day
      What to Pack and What to Leave Behind
      Pre-Cruise Preparations

5. Your Floating Resort — 15
      Exploring the Ship
      Dining Delights
      Staying Entertained

    Making the Most of Sea Days

    Tips for a Smooth Onboard Experience

6. Shore Excursions — 20

    Adventures Await!

        Choosing the Right Excursions

        Making the Most of Each Port

        Exploring on Your Own

        Insider Tips for a Great Day in Port

7. Smooth Sailing — 25

    Overcoming Common Challenges

        Seasickness and How to Avoid It

        Dealing with Cruise Surprises

        Handling Onboard Etiquette

        Making the Most of the Unexpected

8. Making Friends and Memories — 30

        Socializing on a Cruise

        Capturing the Moments

        Capturing the Essence of Your Cruise

9. Disembarkation — 36

    The Journey Home

        Saying Goodbye to the Ship

        The Disembarkation Process

        Getting Home or Continuing Your Journey

        A Smooth Return Home

Introduction
Welcome Aboard!

Welcome aboard, future cruiser! Whether you dream of sun-soaked days on a deck chair, exploring exotic ports, or indulging in gourmet meals at sea, this book is your ticket to smooth sailing. If you've ever found yourself staring wistfully at those majestic ships docked in port and wondered what it's like to be on board, you're in the right place.

Why Cruise?

Let's start with a little secret: Cruising is one of the best-kept secrets in travel. Imagine unpacking your suitcase once and waking up in a new, exciting destination each day—no trains to catch, no driving required, just pure, unadulterated relaxation and adventure. Whether you're looking to explore ancient ruins in Greece, dance the night away in the Caribbean, or sip a cocktail while watching the sunset over the horizon, cruising offers something for everyone.

But cruising isn't just about the destinations but the journey. You're stepping into a world of possibilities from the moment you board. Every day can be as relaxed or as action-packed as you want. Fancy a day of pampering at the spa? You got it. Ready to try your hand at rock climbing or salsa dancing? Go for it! On a cruise, the only limit is your imagination (and maybe your appetite, but we'll get to that later).

Who Is This Book For?

If the thought of your first cruise makes you feel like a fish out of water, don't worry—you're not alone. Whether you're a seasoned traveler or have never set foot on a ship, your first cruise can feel like a giant leap into the unknown. And that's where this book comes in. Consider it your trusty first mate, guiding you through the ins and outs of cruising with a friendly wave and a reassuring smile.

This book is for anyone new to cruising who wants to make the most of their first sea voyage. It's packed with practical tips, insider advice, and a few fun stories to help you avoid common pitfalls and enjoy every moment of your trip. When you finish reading, you'll be ready to confidently walk up the gangway and maybe even a little swagger.

What You'll Discover

Throughout these pages, we'll cover everything you need to know about cruising—from choosing the perfect ship and itinerary to packing like a pro and making the most of your time on board. You'll learn how to navigate the bustling world of cruise lingo (port or starboard, anyone?), avoid rookie mistakes, and embrace all the joys of life at sea.

But this isn't just a guidebook—it's an invitation to a world of adventure. So, let's set sail together on this journey. The ocean is calling, and whether you're dreaming of turquoise waters and white sandy beaches or the cultural treasures of Europe's grand rivers, there's a cruise out there with your name on it. Grab sunscreen, pack your sense of adventure, and prepare to cruise like a pro!

Bon Voyage, and see you on the open seas!

Cruising 101
The Basics

Welcome to the wonderful world of cruising! Before we dive into the details of planning your trip, let's start with the basics. This chapter is your primer on what to expect during your first sea voyage. We'll cover everything from the ship's layout to the flow of a typical day on board, so by the end of this chapter, you'll feel like you've been cruising for years.

What to Expect on Your First Cruise

Picture this: You've just boarded your ship, and as you step into the grand atrium, you're greeted by a dazzling sight—glittering chandeliers, friendly crew members welcoming you with smiles (and maybe a glass of champagne), and fellow passengers milling about, already in vacation mode. You might feel slightly overwhelmed at first, but don't worry; you'll quickly find your sea legs.

The Embarkation Process: The adventure begins before you even set foot on the ship. Embarkation day is when you officially board, and it's a mix of excitement and anticipation. After arriving at the port, you'll check in your luggage (which will magically appear outside your cabin later), go through security, and check in with the cruise line. Then, with your cruise card (your key to everything on board) in hand, you'll step onto the ship for the first time.

Ship Layout: Cruise ships are like floating cities; just like in any city, it's good to know your way around. Ships are divided into decks (like floors in a building), and each deck has attractions—restaurants, pools, theaters, and more. Don't be afraid to explore on your first day. There's usually a handy map available, or you can use the ship's app to find your way. Pro tip: Take a few minutes to locate important spots like the dining room, pool deck, and cabin.

Your Home at Sea: Speaking of cabins, let's talk about your cozy home for the duration of your cruise. Cabins come in all shapes and sizes, from compact interiors to lavish suites with private balconies. Regardless of where you're staying, your cabin will be your retreat—a place to relax after a day of exploring. You'll find all the essentials: a comfortable bed, a bathroom with a shower, storage space, and maybe even a window with an ocean view. Pro tip: Unpack as soon as you can. It helps to make your cabin feel more like home, and it keeps your space neat and tidy.

Daily Schedule: One of the best parts of cruising is that each day can be as active or relaxed as you want. You'll receive a daily schedule (sometimes called a "ship newsletter") delivered to your cabin every evening. This little booklet is vital to the next day's activities, from fitness classes to trivia contests and theater shows to late-night dance parties. Whether you're an early bird or a night owl, there's always something to do.

Cruise Lingo for Newbies

As you embark on your first cruise, you'll quickly realize that cruising has its language—a mix of nautical terms and cruise-specific jargon. Here's a quick crash course to get you up to speed:

- **Port and Starboard:** These are fancy words for left and right when you're facing forward on the ship. "Port" is the left side, and "starboard" is the right. A trick to remember: "Port" and "left" both have four letters.

- **Bow and Stern:** The bow is the front of the ship, and the stern is the back. Simple enough, right?

- **Muster Drill:** Also known as the safety drill, this is a mandatory event before the ship sets sail. You'll learn where your muster station is (your assigned spot in case of an emergency) and get a brief safety briefing. It's a bit like the safety demonstration on a plane but with many more life jackets.

- **Tender:** Some ports are too shallow for the ship to dock, so you'll take a smaller boat, called a tender, to reach the shore. It's a mini-adventure before your main adventure begins!

- **Shore Excursion:** The cruise line offers organized tours and activities at each port. From guided city tours to adrenaline-pumping adventures, there's something for everyone. But don't worry; you can always explore independently if you prefer.

- **Sea Day:** A day spent entirely at sea, with no port stops. Sea days are perfect for exploring the ship, lounging by the pool, or indulging in a spa treatment.

- **Disembarkation:** The sad day when your cruise ends and you leave the ship. But let's not think about that just yet—plenty of fun will be had before then!

Now that you've got the basics down, you're ready to dive into the more exciting aspects of your cruise adventure. In the next chapter, we'll help you choose the perfect cruise for your tastes and budget. From tropical getaways to cultural explorations, the world of cruising is at your fingertips. Let's set sail to find the ideal voyage for you!

Choosing Your Perfect Cruise

So, you're ready to plunge into the world of cruising—exciting. But before you can start imagining yourself lounging on the deck or exploring charming coastal towns, one crucial step is choosing the perfect cruise. With so many options, from destinations to ship sizes and onboard experiences, navigating can feel like a lot. But don't worry, we've got you covered! This chapter is about helping you find that ideal cruise that checks all your boxes.

Finding the Right Cruise for You

First, let's talk about the many types of cruises you can choose from. Like a perfect book for every reader, there's an ideal cruise for every traveler. The trick is figuring out what type of experience you want.

1. Destination, Destination, Destination!

- **Tropical Getaways:** If your idea of heaven is sipping a cocktail on a sandy beach, then a Caribbean or South Pacific cruise might be just what the doctor ordered. Think crystal-clear waters, vibrant coral reefs, and plenty of sunshine.

- **Cultural Explorations:** in Rome, strolling through the streets of Barcelona, or sipping wine in the French countryside.

- For those who love history, art, and local culture, a Mediterranean or European river cruise is a dream. Imagine waking up

- **Adventure Cruises:** Feeling a bit more adventurous? Cruises to Alaska, the Norwegian fjords, or even Antarctica offer breathtaking landscapes and once-in-a-lifetime wildlife encounters. These cruises are perfect for nature lovers and thrill-seekers alike.

- **Bucket List Voyages:** Maybe you've always dreamed of visiting the Far East, South America, or the Middle East. World cruises or long-haul itineraries that cover multiple continents are an incredible way to tick off several dream destinations at once.

2. Ship Size and Style:

- **Mega-Ships:** These floating resorts are the epitome of entertainment, with water parks, Broadway-style shows, dozens of dining options, and activities for all ages. They're perfect for families and anyone who loves a lot of choices.

- **Mid-Size Ships:** Offering a balance of amenities and a more intimate experience, mid-size ships are great for those who want plenty to do but without the crowds. You'll still find various dining options, entertainment, and activities with a more relaxed atmosphere.

- **Small Ships and Yachts:** If you're looking for a more luxurious or personalized experience, small ships and yachts might be your style. These ships often visit less accessible ports and provide a higher crew-to-passenger ratio, ensuring top-notch service. Perfect for travelers who want to escape the hustle and bustle.

- **Specialty Cruises:** If you have a specific interest—music, food and wine, or wellness—there are themed cruises that cater to your passions. These cruises offer specialized activities, guest speakers, and themed excursions around your interest.

3. What's Your Cruise Personality? Let's take a quick personality quiz—no wrong answers here!

- **Are you a relaxer or an explorer?** If you're all about lounging by the pool and catching up on your reading, a cruise with plenty of sea days might be perfect. If you're the type who can't wait to get off the ship and explore new places, look for itineraries with lots of port stops and adventurous excursions.

- **Are you a foodie or a thrill-seeker?** Foodies will love cruises known for their culinary experiences, like those offered by luxury lines or themed food and wine cruises. Thrill-seekers might prefer ships with rock climbing walls, surf simulators, and zip lines.

- **Do you prefer luxury or casual comfort?** Some cruises are about dressing up for dinner and enjoying fine dining, while others are more laid-back with casual dress codes and buffet-style meals. Choose a cruise line that matches your preferred level of formality.

Booking Your Cruise

Now that you've got an idea of what type of cruise you're looking for, it's time to talk about booking. Booking a cruise can be as simple or as detailed as you want, but a little strategy can ensure you get the best deal and the perfect cabin.

1. Timing Is Everything:

- **Early Birds vs. Last-Minute Deals:** Booking early often means you get the pick of the best cabins and sometimes even early booking discounts. However, if you're flexible with dates and destinations, last-minute deals can offer significant savings. Watch cruise line websites or sign up for newsletters to snag these deals.

- **Best Time to Cruise:** The time of year you choose to cruise can affect everything from the weather to the price. Shoulder seasons (just before and after peak season) often offer the best balance of good weather and lower prices. For instance, cruising the Caribbean in late spring or early fall can be less crowded and more affordable.

2. Cabin Fever: Choosing the Perfect Stateroom

- **Inside Cabins:** These are the most budget-friendly options, without windows or natural light. They're perfect if you plan to spend most of your time exploring the ship and ports rather than in your room.

- **Oceanview Cabins:** These cabins, with windows or portholes, offer natural light and ocean views, making them a great mid-range option.

- **Balcony Cabins:** If you love sipping coffee on your private balcony while watching the waves, splurge on a balcony cabin. It's a great way to enjoy some private outdoor space.

- **Suites:** For the ultimate luxury, suites offer the most space, often with separate living areas, larger balconies, and premium amenities. If you're celebrating a special occasion or just want to indulge, a suite is the way to go.

3. All-Inclusive vs. Pay-As-You-Go: Some cruise lines offer all-inclusive packages that cover everything from drinks to shore excursions, while others operate on a pay-as-you-go basis. Decide which approach works best for your budget and preferences. If you like knowing everything is paid for upfront, an all-inclusive option might be more convenient. On the other hand, pay-as-you-go can give you more control over what you spend.

4. Travel Agents vs. DIY Booking: While booking a cruise on your own is possible, working with a travel agent can be a great option, especially for first-timers. Agents can help you navigate the options, secure special perks, and sometimes even offer exclusive discounts. Plus, they assist if anything goes wrong before or during your trip.

With these tips in mind, you're well on your way to selecting the perfect cruise. Remember, the best cruise for you is the one that fits your interests, budget, and style—so take your time exploring the options. In the next chapter, we'll dive into the fun part: getting ready for your adventure! We'll cover everything from packing essentials to pre-cruise preparations to ensure you're fully prepared for smooth sailing.

Preparing for Your Adventure

Ahoy, future cruiser! Now that you've booked your dream cruise, it's time to prepare for the adventure of a lifetime. This chapter is all about the details that will help you prepare for your journey, from packing the perfect suitcase to ensuring you've got all your travel documents in order. Think of this as your pre-cruise checklist, designed to ensure that you'll be cruising into vacation mode when embarkation day arrives with nothing but smooth seas ahead.

Countdown to Cruise Day

Let's kick things off with a fun and practical countdown to your cruise. Consider this your timeline to cruise readiness, breaking down the tasks you'll need to tackle as your departure date approaches.

4-6 Months Before:

- **Check Your Passport:** If your cruise is international, ensure your passport is current. Many countries require that your passport be valid for at least six months beyond your travel dates. If you need a new one, now's the time to apply.

- **Book Your Flights and Accommodations:** If you're flying to the port, book your flights early to get the best deals. Arriving a day before the cruise departs is also a good idea, just in case of flight delays. Consider booking a hotel near the port for a stress-free start to your vacation.

- **Research Shore Excursions:** Now's the time to start thinking about what you want to do at each port. The most popular excursions can sell out, so it's worth booking in advance if you're set on a particular activity.

2-3 Months Before:

- **Plan Your Wardrobe:** Review your cruise itinerary and decide what to pack. Consider the climate of your destinations, any special events or formal nights on board, and the activities you plan to do.

- **Purchase Travel Insurance:** While we hope everything goes smoothly, it's always a good idea to have travel insurance in case of unexpected issues like trip cancellations, medical emergencies, or lost luggage.

- **Check for Vaccinations and Health Requirements:** Depending on where you're cruising, you may need certain vaccinations or health documents. Check with your cruise line and the CDC for any required or recommended vaccinations.

1 Month Before:

- **Review Your Cruise Documents:** You should have received your cruise documents by now, either by mail or electronically. Review everything carefully—your itinerary, boarding passes, and special instructions—to ensure all the details are correct.

- **Start Packing:** Before your trip, pack your suitcase with items you won't need. This could include cruise-specific items like formal wear, swimsuits, and gear for shore excursions.

1 Week Before:

- **Finalize Packing:** Now's the time to pack the rest of your essentials, including toiletries, medications, and travel documents. Don't forget a carry-on bag with a change of clothes, swimwear, and any valuables—you might not get your checked luggage until later on embarkation day.

- **Prepare Your Home:** Make arrangements for pets, plants, and mail. Set any necessary out-of-office messages and ensure your home is secure while you're away.

The Day Before:

- **Double-Check Everything:** Ensure you have all your important documents—passport, boarding pass, insurance details, and any required visas. Charge your devices and pack your chargers and adapters.

- **Get Some Rest:** It's easy to get excited the night before, but try to get a good night's sleep so you're refreshed and ready to enjoy embarkation day.

What to Pack and What to Leave Behind

Packing for a cruise can feel like preparing for a mystery trip—what will you need for formal nights? What about shore excursions? Don't worry; we've got you covered with this packing guide to ensure you're well-prepared for every part of your cruise.

The Essentials:

- **Travel Documents:** The most important items to pack are your passport, cruise documents, travel insurance, and any required visas. Keep these in your carry-on for easy access.

- **Medications and Toiletries:** Bring enough prescription medications to last the entire trip, plus a few extra days, just in case. Don't forget essentials like sunscreen, motion sickness remedies, and a basic first aid kit.

- **Comfortable Clothing:** Pack casual clothing for daytime activities on board and in port. Think shorts, t-shirts, sundresses, and relaxed walking shoes. Don't forget a light jacket or sweater for cooler evenings.

- **Swimwear:** Whether lounging by the pool or snorkeling in the Caribbean, swimwear is a must. Pack at least two swimsuits so you always have a dry one.

- **Formal Attire:** Many cruises have at least one formal night where guests are encouraged to dress up. For men, this could mean a suit or tuxedo, and for women, a cocktail dress or evening gown. Not into dressing up? Some cruise lines offer alternative dining options for those who prefer to keep it casual.

- **Activewear:** If you plan to hit the gym or participate in active shore excursions, bring workout clothes and appropriate footwear.

Extras to Consider:

- **Binoculars:** Great for wildlife spotting or scenic cruising days.

- **Reusable Water Bottle:** Stay hydrated without having to buy bottled water constantly.

- **Power Strip (non-surge protected):** Cruise cabins often have limited outlets, so a power strip can be handy for charging multiple devices.

- **Snorkeling Gear:** If you plan on doing a lot of snorkeling, bringing your own gear can be more comfortable and save on rental costs.

- **Travel-Sized Laundry Detergent:** If you plan to wash clothes during your trip, travel-sized detergent is a lifesaver.

What to Leave Behind:

- **Towels:** Cruise ships provide plenty of towels in your cabin and at the pool.

- **Irons and Steamers** are typically prohibited for safety reasons. Instead, use the ship's laundry service or pack wrinkle-resistant clothing. If left out, the cabin attendant could possibly remove and return the item at the end of the holiday.

- **Too Much Cash:** While having cash for tips and small purchases in port is good, most transactions on board are charged to your cruise card, and credit cards are widely accepted in port.

Pre-Cruise Preparations

Now that your bags are packed and ready, let's discuss a few final preparations to ensure your cruise starts smoothly.

Check-In Online: Most cruise lines allow you to check in online a few weeks before departure. This will speed up the embarkation process and ensure you're ready to board when you arrive at the port.

Print and Organize Your Documents: Even if you have digital copies, printing out your important documents and keeping them in a travel wallet or folder is a good idea. This includes your boarding pass, itinerary, and any shore excursion confirmations.

Download the Cruise Line's App: Many cruise lines offer apps that allow you to check the daily schedule, book dining reservations, and stay in touch with fellow travelers. Download the app before you leave and familiarize yourself with its features.

Research Your Ports of Call: While you might have already booked some shore excursions, doing extra research on your ports of call is worthwhile. Look up maps, learn a few local phrases, and jot down any must-see attractions or restaurants.

Plan Your First Day Onboard: Embarkation day can be a bit hectic, so having a plan can help you make the most of it. Decide whether you want to go to the buffet, explore the ship, or relax by the pool. If you need to make any reservations, such as for specialty dining or spa treatments, it's a good idea to do this as soon as you board.

With your preparations complete, you're ready to embark on your cruise adventure! In the next chapter, we'll dive into what life is like on board your floating resort. From delicious dining options to exciting entertainment, there's much to explore and enjoy. Let's get ready to make the most of every moment at sea!

Your Floating Resort

Congratulations, you've made it! You're officially on board your cruise ship, ready to set sail on a journey of relaxation, adventure, and endless fun. Now that you're here, it's time to explore everything your floating resort offers. From dining delights to endless entertainment, this chapter will guide you through the ins and outs of life on board so you can make the most of every moment.

Exploring the Ship

Stepping onto a cruise ship for the first time feels like entering a wonderland. There's so much to see and do that it's easy to feel overwhelmed—but in the best possible way! The key to making the most of your time on board is to take a little time to explore and get familiar with your surroundings.

The Grand Tour: Stroll around the ship to get your bearings. Grab a deck plan or use the cruise line's app to help you navigate. Explore the different decks, noting where the key areas are located—like the main dining room, pool deck, theaters, and lounges. Pay special attention to areas that catch your eye; these might become your go-to spots for relaxing or socializing.

Hidden Gems: While the main attractions are easy to find, many ships have hidden gems worth seeking. Look for quiet lounges perfect for reading, cozy nooks with ocean views, or secret bars that offer unique drinks and a more intimate atmosphere. Don't be afraid to ask the crew for their favorite spots—they often know the best places to relax away from the crowds.

Safety First: Before you dive into the fun, make sure you attend the mandatory muster drill. This safety briefing is essential to every cruise and will teach you what to do in an emergency. It's quick, easy, and necessary to your cruise experience.

Dining Delights

One of the best parts of cruising is the food—lots and lots of delicious food! From gourmet meals to casual bites, there's something to satisfy every palate. Let's look at the dining options and how to make the most of them.

Main Dining Room: The main dining room is the heart of the ship's dining experience. Here, you'll enjoy multi-course meals prepared by talented chefs. Whether you're craving a juicy steak, fresh seafood, or a decadent dessert, the main dining room has you covered. Dinner is usually served in two seatings—early and late—so you can choose the time that fits your schedule.

Buffet Bonanza: For a more casual dining experience, head to the ship's buffet. The buffet offers various options, from breakfast staples like eggs and bacon to international cuisine, salads, and desserts. It's a great option for grabbing a quick bite or sampling a little bit of everything.

Specialty Restaurants: If you want something unique, consider dining at one of the ship's specialty restaurants. These venues offer themed dining experiences like Italian trattorias, sushi bars, or steakhouses. While there's usually an additional fee, the food and atmosphere are often worth the splurge. Make reservations early, as these spots can fill up quickly.

Room Service: Feeling a bit lazy or craving a midnight snack? Most cruise ships offer room service, allowing you to enjoy a meal or snack from the comfort of your cabin. Room service menus vary, but you can usually find a selection of sandwiches, salads, and desserts. Best of all, it's often available 24/7, so you can satisfy your cravings anytime.

Dietary Needs: Cruise lines are very accommodating regarding dietary restrictions. Whether you're vegetarian, gluten-free, or have food allergies, just let the dining staff know, and they'll ensure you have delicious options that meet your needs.

Staying Entertained

When it comes to entertainment, cruise ships genuinely shine. There's always something happening on board, whether you're in the mood for a Broadway-style show, a lively dance party, or a quiet movie night under the stars. Let's dive into how you can stay entertained at sea.

Theater Shows: One of the highlights of any cruise is the nightly entertainment in the main theater. Depending on the ship, you might be treated to Broadway-style musicals, comedy acts, magic shows, or even acrobatic performances. The shows are usually family-friendly and free of charge, making them a great way to end the evening.

Live Music: If you love music, you're in luck. Cruise ships are filled with live music, from piano bars and jazz lounges to poolside bands and DJs. Whether you want to dance the night away or relax with a cocktail while listening to smooth tunes, there's a spot on board for every music lover.

Casinos and Nightclubs: For those who enjoy a bit of nightlife, many cruise ships have casinos where you can try your luck at the slots or gaming tables. If dancing is more your style, head to the nightclub to dance to the latest hits. Just remember to pace yourself—tomorrow is another day of fun!

Movies Under the Stars: Imagine watching your favorite movie under a blanket of stars with the ocean as your backdrop. Many ships offer outdoor movie screenings, complete with popcorn and cozy blankets. It's a magical way to spend an evening and a perfect family-friendly activity.

Daytime Fun: During the day, the entertainment continues with poolside games, trivia contests, dance classes, and more. You might join a cooking demonstration, try your hand at shuffleboard, or even compete in a belly flop contest! Each evening, the daily schedule delivered to your cabin will list all the activities so you can plan your day accordingly.

Spa and Fitness: If relaxation and wellness are high, head to the ship's spa for a massage, facial, or other pampering treatments. Many ships also have fully equipped fitness centers with ocean views and yoga and fitness classes. Book a spa day for an indulgent experience, and let all your cares melt away.

Making the Most of Sea Days

Sea days—those glorious days when the ship is sailing between ports—are your time to enjoy everything the ship offers. Whether you're an early riser or prefer to sleep in, there's no right or wrong way to spend a sea day. Here are some ideas to help you make the most of your time.

Relax by the Pool: Sea days are perfect for lounging by the pool, soaking up the sun, and cooling off with a dip. Find a comfy deck chair, order a fruity drink, and let the relaxation begin. If you prefer a quieter spot, look for the adults-only pool area or a secluded sundeck.

Attend a Workshop or Class: Many cruise lines offer a variety of workshops and classes on sea days. You might learn to salsa dance, improve your photography skills, or even participate in a wine tasting. It's a great way to try something new and meet fellow passengers with similar interests.

Indulge in a Spa Day: There's no better time to treat yourself to a spa day than on a sea day. Book a massage, unwind in the sauna, or relax in the spa's tranquil lounge. Some ships even offer special spa packages for sea days, so watch for deals.

Explore the Ship: Sea days are the perfect opportunity to explore parts of the ship you might have missed. Visit the onboard shops, check out the art gallery, or take a leisurely walk around the deck. If you're feeling adventurous, try a new activity, like rock climbing or surfing (on ships with these amenities).

Enjoy a Leisurely Meal: With no port calls on the schedule, sea days are ideal for enjoying a leisurely meal. Take your time at breakfast, linger over lunch, or indulge in afternoon tea. It's a chance to savor the delicious food without feeling rushed.

Take in the Views: Don't forget to spend some time simply enjoying the views. Whether gazing out at the endless horizon or watching for dolphins, there's something incredibly peaceful about being at sea. Grab coffee or wine, find a quiet spot, and let the ocean work magic.

Tips for a Smooth Onboard Experience

To wrap up this chapter, here are a few additional tips to ensure your time on board is as smooth and enjoyable as possible:

- **Stay Hydrated:** It's easy to forget to drink enough water, especially if you're busy enjoying the fun. Keep a reusable water bottle with you, and stay hydrated throughout the day.

- **Mind the Dress Code:** Some cruise lines have dress codes for certain restaurants or events, especially on formal nights. Check the daily schedule or ask a crew member if you're unsure what to wear.

- **Settle into a Routine:** A little routine can go a long way while on vacation. Establishing a daily pattern—like morning coffee on the balcony or an evening stroll on the deck—can help you feel more at home on board.

- **Be Social:** Don't be shy about conversing with fellow passengers or crew members. Cruising is a social experience, and you might make some new friends along the way.

- **Relax and Enjoy:** Above all, remember that this is your vacation. Whether you're packing your days with activities or doing nothing, the most important thing is enjoying yourself. So kick back, relax, and let the waves carry you to new adventures.

Now that you're familiar with life on board, you're ready to embrace the cruise experience fully. In the next chapter, we'll dive into the exciting world of shore.

Shore Excursions
Adventures Await!

While life on board your cruise ship is a world of its own, one of the most thrilling aspects of cruising is the opportunity to explore new and exciting destinations. Each port of call offers a unique experience, from historic cities and charming villages to pristine beaches and breathtaking natural wonders. This chapter is all about making the most of your time on shore, whether you are planning to take part in organized excursions or venture out on your own.

Choosing the Right Excursions

Choosing suitable shore excursions can feel overwhelming, with many exciting possibilities at each port. Should you go for an action-packed adventure, a cultural tour, or a relaxing day at the beach? Here's how to decide what's best for you.

1. **Know Your Interests:** Start by thinking about what excites you most. Are you a history buff who loves exploring ancient ruins and historic sites? Or perhaps you're a nature lover eager to hike through lush landscapes or snorkel in crystal-clear waters? Maybe you're all about trying new foods and immersing yourself in local culture. Identifying your interests will help you narrow down the options.

2. **Consider Your Energy Levels:** While booking multiple excursions in every port is tempting, remember that vacation should also be about relaxation. Be honest about how much activity you want to take on each day. Some excursions are full-day adventures with lots of walking or physical activity, while others are more leisurely, allowing you to take in the sights at a slower pace.

3. **Do Your Research:** Before booking, take some time to research the excursions available at each port. Cruise lines often describe each excursion, including the duration, level of physical activity, and what's included. You can also find reviews online from past cruisers, giving you a good sense of what to expect.

4. **Think About Timing:** Consider how much time you'll have in each port and plan accordingly. A short, well-organized excursion might be best if your ship is only docked for a few hours. On the other hand, if you have a full day to explore, you can opt for a more in-depth experience or even combine a couple of shorter activities.

5. **Book Early, But Stay Flexible:** Popular excursions can sell out quickly, so it's a good idea to book in advance, especially if there's something you don't want to miss. However, remember that plans can change due to weather, ship schedules, or simply a change of heart. Most cruise lines allow you to modify or cancel excursions up to a certain point before the trip, so stay flexible and open to new opportunities.

Making the Most of Each Port

Whether you've booked a guided tour or plan to explore independently, each port of call is a chance to dive into a new world. Here's how to ensure you get the most out of every destination.

1. **Arrive Prepared:** Before you step off the ship, take a few minutes to review the day's itinerary and any excursion details. Ensure you have everything you need—your cruise card, ID, tickets, and essentials like sunscreen, a hat, and comfortable shoes. Bringing some local currency is also a good idea, as not all vendors may accept credit cards.

2. **Get an Early Start:** If you plan to explore independently, try to disembark early to beat the crowds. This gives you a head start on popular attractions and lets you experience the destination more leisurely. Plus, the earlier you start, the more time you'll have to explore before returning to the ship.

3. **Embrace Local Culture:** One of the most rewarding aspects of

travel is immersing yourself in the local culture. Take the time to learn a few basic phrases in the local language, try traditional foods, and interact with locals. Whether browsing a market, visiting a historic site, or simply enjoying a cup of coffee at a café, these experiences will give you a deeper connection to the places you visit.

4. **Capture the Moment:** Don't forget to document your adventures! Whether you're an avid photographer or just snapping shots with your phone, capturing the beauty and uniqueness of each destination will help preserve your memories long after the cruise. Consider creating a travel journal or blog where you can jot down your thoughts and experiences each day.

5. **Stay Safe and Be Aware:** While exploring new places is exciting, it's essential to stay aware of your surroundings and prioritize safety. Stick to well-lit, populated areas, especially if you're venturing out on your own. Be mindful of local customs and dress codes, and secure your belongings. And, of course, always keep an eye on the time—missing the ship's departure is one adventure you definitely want to avoid!

6. **Have a Plan B:** Sometimes things don't go as planned—an excursion might be canceled due to weather, or you might decide to relax rather than explore. It's always good to have a backup plan. Whether that means enjoying the ship's amenities while everyone else is ashore or simply wandering around the port town at your own pace, having a flexible attitude will ensure you still have a great day, no matter what.

Exploring on Your Own

While organized shore excursions are a convenient way to experience a destination, something must be said before you can strike out alone. Here's how to plan your self-guided adventure.

1. **Do Your Homework:** Before your cruise, research the ports of call to identify must-see attractions, local restaurants, and other points of interest. Websites, travel blogs, and guidebooks can provide valuable insights and tips. You might also want to

download maps or apps to help you navigate once you're on land.

2. **Use Public Transportation:** Public transportation is an affordable and efficient way to get around in many ports. Whether it's a bus, tram, or metro, local transport can take you to famous sites without needing a pricey taxi. Just understand the routes and schedules so you don't miss your ride back to the ship.

3. **Take a Walking Tour:** Walking is one of the best ways to explore a new place, and many cities offer free or low-cost walking tours led by knowledgeable locals. These tours often cover significant attractions and hidden gems, giving you a more intimate look at the destination.

4. **Enjoy a Leisurely Day:** Sometimes, the best way to experience a port is simply to wander and see where the day takes you. Browse local shops, relax at a café, or find a quiet park to enjoy the scenery. If your ship is docked for an extended period, you might have time to explore at your own pace and then return to the ship for a relaxing afternoon by the pool.

5. **Be Back On Time:** While exploring independently offers freedom and flexibility, keeping an eye on the clock is crucial. The ship won't wait for latecomers, so allow plenty of time to return to the port. Aim to return to the ship at least an hour before the scheduled departure to be safe. Especially if it is a tender port, Do not wait until the last tender.

Insider Tips for a Great Day in Port

To wrap up this chapter, here are a few insider tips that will help you make the most of your shore excursions and port days:

- **Pack Light:** When heading ashore, carry only what you need. A small backpack or crossbody bag is perfect for holding essentials like your cruise card, wallet, phone, and camera. Keep it light so you can move around quickly and enjoy your day.

- **Dress Appropriately:** When choosing your outfit for the day, consider the weather and local customs. Comfortable walking shoes are a must, especially if you'll be on your feet for long periods. A hat and sunglasses are also essential for sunny days.

- **Stay Hydrated and Snack Smart:** It's easy to get caught up in the excitement of exploring and forget to eat and drink. Bring a reusable water bottle and refill it throughout the day. Carry a small snack, like a granola bar or fruit, to keep your energy up between meals.

- **Use the Ship's Concierge:** If you have questions about the port or need recommendations for activities or dining, the ship's concierge can be a valuable resource. They often have insider knowledge about the best places to visit and can help with last-minute bookings.

- **Don't Stress About the Crowds:** Ports can get busy, especially when multiple ships are docked simultaneously. If you want to avoid the crowds, consider visiting less popular attractions or venturing further afield. Alternatively, embrace the hustle and bustle as part of the experience—after all, you're there to have fun!

With these tips and insights, you're well-prepared to make the most of your shore excursions and port days. Whether exploring ancient ruins, relaxing on a tropical beach, or discovering a new city, every stop on your cruise is an opportunity for adventure and discovery. In the next chapter, we'll tackle some common challenges you might encounter on a cruise and how to overcome them easily. Smooth sailing awaits!

Smooth Sailing
Overcoming Common Challenges

While cruising is often a dream vacation filled with relaxation and adventure, like any trip, it can come with its own challenges. Whether dealing with seasickness, navigating unexpected changes in your itinerary, or simply figuring out how to handle the buffet line, this chapter is here to help you sail through any bumps in the road with ease and a smile.

Seasickness and How to Avoid It

One of the most common concerns for first-time cruisers is seasickness. The good news is that modern cruise ships are equipped with stabilizers that minimize motion, making seasickness less of an issue than it used to be. But if you're prone to motion sickness or just want to be prepared, here are some tips to keep those queasy feelings at bay.

1. **Choose Your Cabin Wisely:** If you're worried about seasickness, consider booking a cabin on a lower deck in the middle of the ship. This area tends to be the most stable, with less noticeable motion. Avoid cabins at the ship's very front (bow) or back (stern), where movement can be more pronounced.

2. **Take Preventative Measures:** If you know you're prone to motion sickness, start taking over-the-counter medication, such as Dramamine or Bonine, a day before you board the ship. These medications are most effective when taken preventatively rather than waiting until symptoms start. Non-drowsy formulas are available so you can enjoy your day without feeling sleepy.

3. **Try Natural Remedies:** Ginger is a well-known remedy for nausea for those who prefer a natural approach. You can take ginger in various forms—capsules, ginger ale, or ginger

candies. Another popular option is acupressure wristbands, like Sea-Bands, which apply pressure to a point on your wrist that's believed to help reduce nausea.

4. **Watch What You Eat and Drink:** If you feel a bit off, avoid heavy, greasy, or spicy foods that might upset your stomach. Instead, stick to light, bland meals. Staying hydrated is also important, but try to limit alcohol and caffeine, which can dehydrate you and potentially make seasickness worse.

5. **Get Fresh Air and Focus on the Horizon:** If you start to feel queasy, head outside and get some fresh air. Focusing on the horizon, where the sea meets the sky, can help your body adjust to the motion. Sit or lie down with your head elevated and close your eyes to minimize sensory input.

6. **Don't Stress:** Worrying about seasickness can sometimes make it worse. Stay calm and remind yourself that most people adjust to the ship's motion after the first day. If you do feel sick, the ship's medical staff is available to help, and they often have stronger medications on hand if needed.

Note on this: I personally, when I was younger, would suffer from this quite badly, and I was worried about this before I started to cruise. But because of the ships' size and stability, the thought of sea sickness became a distant memory, allowing me to enjoy the ship's experience truly.

Dealing with Cruise Surprises

Even with the best planning, cruises can come with a few surprises—some delightful, others less so. Here's how to handle some of the most common cruise curveballs with grace and good humor.

1. **Weather Changes:** Mother Nature doesn't always cooperate with our vacation plans. While cruise lines do their best to stick to the itinerary, sometimes weather conditions require changes, such as skipping a port or adjusting the route. If this happens, remember that safety comes first. Use any extra sea days to explore the ship's amenities or join onboard activities. The crew often goes above and beyond to add extra entertainment when plans change.

2. **Missed Ports:** Occasionally, rough seas or other conditions may prevent the ship from docking at a scheduled port. While this can be disappointing, keeping a positive attitude is essential. The cruise line may offer alternative activities, and you might even receive a refund or onboard credit for any excursions you booked. Use the unexpected free time to relax, enjoy the ship's offerings, or get to know your fellow passengers better.

3. **Cabin Issues:** Don't hesitate to contact guest services if you encounter a problem with your cabin—whether it's a noisy neighbor, a plumbing issue, or something else. The crew is there to ensure you have a comfortable stay, and they're usually quick to resolve any issues. If the problem persists, politely request to speak with a supervisor or see if an alternative cabin is available.

4. **Lost Luggage:** If your luggage is delayed or lost, notify the cruise line immediately. They often have a plan to help, such as providing basic toiletries or even a small onboard credit to purchase essentials. Packing a change of clothes and a swimsuit in your carry-on bag is also a good idea so you're prepared even if your luggage is delayed.

5. **Health Concerns:** While most people stay healthy on cruises, it's essential to take precautions, especially regarding hygiene. Wash your hands frequently, use hand sanitizer stations around the ship, and avoid touching your face. If you do start feeling unwell, visit the ship's medical center. The staff is trained to handle various medical issues, and seeking help early is better. Usually, medical staff are onboard the ship to seek advice if they are concerned.

6. **Overcoming Language Barriers:** If your cruise takes you to non-English-speaking countries, you might encounter language barriers. While most tourist areas have English-speaking staff, learning a few key phrases in the local language can go a long way. Carrying a translation app or phrasebook can also be helpful. And remember, a friendly smile and a little patience can bridge many gaps!

Handling Onboard Etiquette

Cruise ships are like small floating communities; a little courtesy can make everyone's experience more enjoyable. Here's a quick guide to onboard etiquette.

1. **Poolside Manners:** Pool decks can get crowded on sea days, so be considerate of your fellow passengers. Avoid "chair hogging" (reserving chairs with towels or belongings) if you're not planning to use them soon. If you're leaving the pool area for more than 30 minutes, it's best to free up your chair for someone else.

2. **Dress Code Awareness:** While cruise ships are generally relaxed environments, certain areas or events may have specific dress codes, especially during formal nights. Adhering to these dress codes helps maintain the atmosphere of the event. If you prefer a casual experience, check the daily schedule for alternative dining or entertainment options.

3. **Elevator Etiquette:** With so many people on board, elevators can get busy, especially around mealtimes and showtimes. If you're able, consider taking the stairs to free up the elevator for those who need it more. When using the elevator, let others exit before entering, and if it's complete, wait for the next one.

4. **Be Respectful of Quiet Spaces:** Many ships have designated quiet zones or adults-only areas. These are perfect spots for reading, napping, or simply enjoying some peace and quiet. Respect the atmosphere by keeping noise to a minimum and silencing your phone.

5. **Tipping and Gratuities:** Most cruise lines include gratuities in your onboard account, but it's still nice to show appreciation to crew members who go above and beyond. If someone has made your cruise particularly special—whether it's your cabin steward, a favorite bartender, or a dining room server—consider giving them a small additional tip or a kind note.

6. **Respecting Personal Space:** Cruise ships are social environments, but respecting others' personal space is essential.

If you're sharing a table with strangers, engage in friendly conversation, but be mindful if they seem to prefer quiet. Be patient and courteous in crowded areas like the buffet or theater.

Making the Most of the Unexpected

Sometimes, the unexpected moments on a cruise can be the most memorable. Maybe you'll make new friends while waiting out a storm, discover a hidden talent at a shipboard contest, or stumble upon a secluded deck where you can watch the sunset peacefully. The key is to stay flexible, keep a positive attitude, and embrace the adventure—even when things don't go as planned.

1. **Embrace the Journey:** Remember, cruising is as much about the journey as it is about the destination. If plans change or something doesn't go as expected, try to see it as part of the adventure. Every cruise has its share of surprises, and how you handle them can make all the difference.

2. **Make New Friends:** Some of the best cruise memories come from the people you meet. Whether it's fellow passengers or the ship's crew, take the time to connect with others. You might make lifelong friends or at least have some great conversations that add to the richness of your experience.

3. **Take It Easy:** Cruises are meant to be relaxing, so don't sweat the small stuff. If something goes wrong, take a deep breath and focus on the positives. You're on vacation, after all, and there's always something fun to do or a new place to explore.

4. **Learn Something New:** If an excursion is canceled or you have unexpected free time, use it to try something new. Join a cooking class, attend a lecture, or learn a new dance step. You never know what new interests you might discover.

With these strategies in hand, you're ready to handle whatever your cruise may throw your way. In the next chapter, we'll explore how to make lasting memories on your cruise—whether through photography, journaling, or simply soaking in every moment. Let's make sure your cruise is one you'll never forget!

Making Friends and Memories

One of the most beautiful aspects of cruising is the opportunity to create lasting memories with the people you travel with and the new friends you make along the way. From capturing the perfect sunset photo to sharing stories over dinner, this chapter will guide you in making your cruise experience truly unforgettable.

Socializing on a Cruise

Cruising is an incredibly social activity. Whether traveling solo, with a partner, or in a group, you'll find plenty of opportunities to meet new people and make friends. Here's how to break the ice and connect with fellow passengers and crew members.

1. **Embrace Shared Experiences:** One of the easiest ways to meet people on a cruise is by participating in shared activities. These events unite people, from trivia games to dance classes. Don't be shy—join in, have fun, and you'll likely chat with fellow participants before you know it.

2. **Take Advantage of Group Dining:** Most cruises offer communal dining options where you can share a table with other passengers. This is a fantastic way to meet people, exchange travel stories, and connect over a delicious meal. If you're uncomfortable with group dining, consider starting with more casual venues like buffets or poolside grills, where the atmosphere is relaxed and conversation flows easily.

3. **Attend Social Events:** Cruises often host social events designed explicitly for mingling, such as welcome parties, themed nights, or meet-and-greet gatherings. These events are great places to

introduce yourself to other cruisers and find people with similar interests. Look out for events like "Singles Meetups," "Wine Tastings," or "Deck Parties," which can offer relaxed settings for making new friends.

4. **Strike-Up Conversations:** One of the beauties of cruising is that everyone is on vacation and generally in a great mood. Don't be afraid to converse with someone while waiting in line, sitting by the pool, or enjoying a show. A simple "Where are you from?" or "Is this your first cruise?" can start a friendly chat that leads to a new friendship.

5. **Connect with the Crew:** The ship's crew members are often seasoned travelers with fascinating stories to share. Take the time to chat with your cabin steward, bartenders, or activity leaders. You will learn more about life on board and get insider tips on the best things to do and see during your cruise.

Capturing the Moments

Memories are precious, and there are many ways to capture the special moments of your cruise. Whether you're into photography, journaling, or collecting souvenirs, here are some ideas to help you preserve the magic of your journey.

1. Photography Tips for Cruisers: Taking great photos on a cruise is all about timing, light, and composition. Here are a few tips to ensure you capture stunning images:

- **Golden Hour Magic:** The best time to take photos is during the "golden hour," shortly after sunrise or just before sunset. The soft, warm light creates beautiful, flattering tones, making your photos look almost magical. Whether you're capturing the ship's deck, a coastal town, or a portrait of your travel companions, this light will enhance your images.

- **Tell a Story:** Try to capture a narrative with your photos. Start with a shot of the ship as you embark, followed by images of your cabin, meals, activities, and shore excursions. By the end of the trip, you'll have a visual diary that tells the story of your cruise from start to finish.

- **Use the Rule of Thirds:** For balanced and visually appealing photos, use the rule of thirds. Imagine your frame is divided into nine equal squares (like a tic-tac-toe grid), and position the most critical elements of your scene along these lines or at their intersections. Most cameras and phones have a grid setting to help you with this.

- **Get Candid:** Some of the best photos are the ones you don't plan. Capture candid moments—your partner laughing, your kids playing in the pool, or a fellow passenger enjoying the view. These shots often evoke the most emotion when you look back on them.

- **Don't Forget the Details:** While focusing on the big picture is easy, don't forget to photograph the little details that make your cruise unique. The color of the water, the intricate design of a meal, or the texture of the ship's railing can all add depth to your photo collection.

2. Keeping a Travel Journal: Travel journals are a fantastic way to document your thoughts, feelings, and experiences during your cruise. Here's how to get started:

- **Start with a Pre-Cruise Entry:** Write about your excitement, any pre-cruise preparations, and your expectations for the trip. This entry will be fun to remember once you've experienced the cruise.

- **Daily Reflections:** Set aside a few minutes daily to jot down highlights, exciting encounters, and your favorite moments. Include details like the sights you saw, the foods you tried, and the people you met. Even a few sentences can help capture the essence of your day.

- **Incorporate Mementos:** Attach small mementos, such as ticket stubs, maps, or postcards, to your journal entries. These physical items will add a tactile dimension to your memories.

- **Express Yourself:** Don't feel confined to just writing. Draw sketches, doodle, or include pressed flowers or leaves from your excursions. Your journal is your creative space, so make it your own.

3. Collecting Souvenirs: Bringing home a piece of your cruise is a great way to keep the memories alive. Here are some ideas for meaningful souvenirs:

- **Local Crafts:** Look for handmade items from the places you visit. These could be anything from jewelry and pottery to textiles and art. Not only do they support local artisans, but they also serve as unique reminders of your journey.

- **Photobooks:** Once you're back home, consider creating a photobook that compiles your favorite images from the cruise. Many online services allow you to design custom books with captions, maps, and other personal touches.

- **Custom Postcards:** Write a postcard to yourself from each port of call, describing your day and any memorable moments. Mail them home, and you'll have a series of mini travelogues to look back on when they arrive.

- **Small Keepsakes:** Collect small, inexpensive items like shells, pebbles, or coins from each destination. Display them in a shadow box or jar to remind you of your travels.

4. Sharing Your Experience: Once your cruise is over, sharing your experience with others can be a great way to relive the memories. Consider these options:

- **Create a Travel Blog:** If you enjoy writing and photography, start a travel blog to document your cruise adventures. It's a great way to share tips and stories with friends, family, and fellow travelers.

- **Social Media Albums:** Create an album on your social media platforms to share your cruise photos with your network. Add captions highlighting special moments, and tag your travel companions to keep the memories alive.

- **Plan a Post-Cruise Get-Together:** Host a small gathering with the friends you made on the cruise or with those you traveled with. Share photos, swap stories, and reminisce about the highlights of your trip.

Capturing the Essence of Your Cruise

While photos and souvenirs are lovely, sometimes the best way to remember your cruise is simply to be present and soak in the experience. Here's how to make sure you fully appreciate each moment.

1. **Slow Down and Savor:** It's easy to get caught up in the excitement of activities and excursions, but don't forget to slow down and savor the quiet moments. Whether watching the sunrise from your balcony, enjoying a leisurely breakfast on the deck, or feeling the breeze as you sail into a new port, take the time to appreciate these simple pleasures.

2. **Reflect and Appreciate:** At the end of each day, take a few moments to reflect on what you've experienced. Think about what made you smile, what surprised you, and what you're grateful for. These reflections will help cement the memories in your mind and allow you to carry the joy of your cruise long after it's over.

3. **Be Open to New Experiences:** Sometimes, the best memories come from stepping out of your comfort zone. Whether trying a new dish, joining an activity you wouldn't normally consider, or striking up a conversation with a stranger, embrace the opportunities for new experiences. You might just discover something extraordinary.

4. **Enjoy the Journey:** Remember that a cruise is about the destination and the journey itself. The time you spend on the ship, the people you meet, and the experiences you have along the way make cruising so special. Embrace every aspect of the journey, and you'll find that the memories you create are even more prosperous and more meaningful.

As your cruise adventure ends, you'll be left with a treasure trove of memories—new friends, unforgettable experiences, and stories to share for years to come. In the final chapter, we'll guide you through the disembarkation process and help you transition back to life on land, ensuring that the end of your cruise is just as smooth and enjoyable as the rest of your journey.

Disembarkation
The Journey Home

As your cruise adventure nears its end, it's time to start thinking about disembarkation—leaving the ship and transitioning back to life on land. While saying goodbye to your floating home can be bittersweet, this chapter will help ensure your final day is as smooth and stress-free as possible. We'll guide you through the disembarkation process, offer tips for making the most of your last hours on board, and help you manage those post-cruise blues.

Saying Goodbye to the Ship

Your last day on board is a chance to savor every moment and tie up any loose ends before you disembark. Here's how to make the most of it.

1. Packing Up One of the first tasks on your final day is packing your belongings. Most cruise lines will ask you to place your luggage outside your cabin the night before disembarkation so it can be collected and transported off the ship. Here's how to make packing as painless as possible:

- **Start Early:** Don't wait until the last minute to pack. Start organizing your things the day before so you're not rushing at night. Begin by packing items you won't need for your final evening or morning on board, such as formal wear, extra shoes, and souvenirs.

- **Keep Essentials Handy:** Since your checked luggage will be collected the night before, pack a small carry-on bag with essentials for your last day. This should include your travel documents, a change of clothes, toiletries, medications, and any valuables.

- **Double-Check:** Before sealing your suitcase, quickly sweep your cabin to ensure you haven't left anything behind. Check drawers, closets, and the bathroom. Don't forget to look under the bed and in the safe.

2. Settling Your Onboard Account: Throughout your cruise, you've likely charged various purchases to your onboard account, such as drinks, spa treatments, and shore excursions. On your final day, you must settle this account before disembarking.

- **Review Your Statement:** On the last night of your cruise, you'll receive an itemized statement of your charges, either delivered to your cabin or available via the ship's app. Take the time to review it carefully to ensure everything is correct.

- **Resolve Any Discrepancies:** If you notice discrepancies or charges you don't recognize, visit the guest services desk as soon as possible to resolve them. It's much easier to address these issues before you leave the ship.

- **Payment:** If you've linked a credit card to your onboard account, your charges will be automatically billed to your card. If you prefer to pay with cash or a different method, visit guest services to settle your account before disembarking.

3. Enjoying Your Final Evening: Your last night on the ship is the perfect time to reflect on your cruise and enjoy one more evening of fun and relaxation.

- **A Farewell:** Many cruise lines offer special farewell dinners on the last night, featuring favorite dishes from the voyage or a special menu. Take this opportunity to dress up, savor the cuisine, and toast to the beautiful memories you've made.

- **One Last Show:** If there's an evening show you haven't seen yet, now's your chance! Whether it's a musical performance, comedy show, or other entertainment, make the most of your final night on board.

- **Stroll Under the Stars:** Take a leisurely stroll on deck after dinner. Enjoy the night air, gaze at the stars, and soak in the last moments of being at sea. It's a beautiful way to say goodbye to the ship and reflect on your journey.

The Disembarkation Process

Disembarkation day can be a bit hectic, but you can navigate it smoothly with a little preparation. Here's what to expect and how to make the process as stress-free as possible.

1. Morning of Disembarkation: On the morning of disembarkation, you must vacate your cabin by a specific time, usually around 8:00 AM. However, you don't have to leave the ship immediately—most cruise lines allow you to enjoy breakfast and relax in designated areas until it's your turn to disembark.

- **Breakfast:** Start your day with a leisurely breakfast in the main dining room or buffet. It's your last chance to enjoy the ship's culinary offerings, so take your time and savor the meal.

- **Final Preparations:** After breakfast, return to your cabin to grab your carry-on bag and do one last check to ensure you haven't left anything behind. Leave your cabin in good order for the next guests.

- **Waiting Areas:** Once you've vacated your cabin, head to one of the designated waiting areas on the ship. This could be a lounge, the theater, or another comfortable spot where you can relax until your group is called to disembark.

2. Disembarkation Groups: Disembarkation is usually organized by groups based on factors such as your deck, loyalty status, or whether you have an early flight. You'll receive a disembarkation number or color-coded luggage tag that corresponds to your group.

- **Listen for Announcements:** Check out announcements over the ship's PA system or check the ship's app to know when your group is called. Once it's your turn, gather your belongings and proceed to the gangway.

- **Immigration and Customs:** Depending on the port and your itinerary, you may need to go through immigration and customs as you disembark. Have your passport and travel documents ready, and follow the signs or crew instructions to the appropriate area.

3. Collecting Your Luggage: After disembarking, you'll enter the cruise terminal where your luggage awaits. The luggage is typically arranged by color-coded tags or group numbers, making it easier to find your bags.

- **Baggage Claim:** Locate your group's section and retrieve your luggage. If you can't find your bags, ask a staff member for assistance.

- **Customs Inspection:** After collecting your luggage, you may need to go through customs inspection in some ports. Be prepared to declare any purchases or items you've brought back and follow the instructions of customs officers.

Getting Home or Continuing Your Journey

Once you've successfully disembarked and collected your luggage, it's time to head home or continue your travels. Here's how to make your post-cruise transition as smooth as possible.

1. Arranging Transportation: Before your cruise ends, make sure you've arranged transportation from the port to the airport, your hotel, or home.

- **Cruise Line Transfers:** Many cruise lines offer shuttle services to the airport or nearby hotels. These can be a convenient option, especially if unfamiliar with the area.

- **Taxis and Rideshares:** Taxis and rideshare services like Uber or Lyft are usually available at the port, but there can be a wait, especially during peak disembarkation times. If you're in a hurry, consider pre-booking a private transfer.

- **Public Transportation:** In some cities, public transportation options like buses, trains, or metro systems are available from the port. Research your options ahead of time if you plan to use public transit.

2. Managing Post-Cruise Blues: After an amazing cruise, feeling a little down is normal when it's time to return to your regular routine. Here's how to keep the post-cruise blues at bay:

- **Plan Your Next Trip:** One of the best ways to beat the post-vacation slump is to start planning your next adventure! Whether it's another cruise or a different type of trip, having something to look forward to can lift your spirits.

- **Stay in Touch with Cruise Friends:** If you made friends on your cruise, stay connected! Exchange contact information before disembarking and keep in touch via email or social media. You might even plan to cruise together again in the future.

- **Relive the Memories:** Take some time to organize your photos, write in your travel journal, or create a scrapbook of your cruise. Sharing your experiences with friends and family can also help you relive the fun.

- **Ease Back into Routine:** Give yourself a day or two to ease back into your routine. Unpack, do laundry, and take care of any post-cruise tasks leisurely. This will help you transition back to reality without feeling overwhelmed.

3. Reflecting on Your Journey: As you settle back into everyday life, take a moment to reflect on your cruise experience. What were your favorite moments? What did you learn about yourself? How did the trip impact you? These reflections can help you appreciate the journey even more and carry the positive energy of your cruise into your daily life.

A Smooth Return Home

Returning home after a cruise doesn't have to be a letdown. With a little planning and the right mindset, you can transition smoothly and carry the joy of your cruise long after the ship has docked.

1. **Unpacking Tips:** When you get home, resist the urge to leave your suitcase in the corner. Unpack promptly so you can fully settle back in. As you unpack, take the time to admire any souvenirs you brought back and reminisce about the places you

visited.

2. **Share Your Experiences:** Catch up with friends and family, share your cruise stories, and show off your favorite photos. Not only will this help you relive the adventure, but it might also inspire others to consider cruising for their next vacation.

3. **Self-Care After Travel:** Travel can be tiring, so give yourself some time to rest and recharge. A warm bath, a good night's sleep, or a relaxing day at home can do wonders for helping you feel refreshed and ready to jump back into your routine.

4. **Keep the Spirit Alive:** Finally, don't let the cruise spirit fade away. Stay connected to the joy of travel by learning more about the destinations you visited, cooking some of the dishes you enjoyed on board, or even planning a themed night at home that brings a bit of the cruise experience into your everyday life.

As your journey comes to an end, remember that every cruise is more than just a vacation—it's an opportunity to explore, learn, and grow. You've not only traveled to new places but also created lasting memories, made new friends, and perhaps even discovered something new about yourself. As you step off the ship and return to your everyday life, take with you the spirit of adventure, the joy of exploration, and the sense of relaxation that only a cruise can provide.

Until your next voyage, happy sailing!

Printed in Great Britain
by Amazon